riverfall

Simmons B. Buntin

salmonpoetry

Published in 2005 by
Salmon Publishing,
Cliffs of Moher, County Clare, Ireland
Website: www.salmonpoetry.com
email: info@salmonpoetry.com

Copyright © Simmons B. Buntin, 2005

ISBN 1 903392 47 0

All rights reserved. No part of this publication may be reproduced or transmitted in any form or by any means, electronic or mechanical, including photography, recording, or any information storage or retrieval system, without permission in writing from the publisher. The book is sold subject to the condition that it shall not, by way of trade or otherwise, be lent, resold or otherwise circulated without the publisher's prior consent in any form of binding or cover other than that in which it is published and without a similar condition, including this condition, being imposed on the subsequent purchaser.

Cover artwork & design: Markus Beaumonte
Typesetting: Siobhán Hutson

For my girls:

Billie, Ann-Elise, Juliet

Acknowledgments

Special thanks to Rod Smith, Miriam Clark, and Jessie Lendennie. Thanks also to those who have published these poems in one format or another:

"A Gathering" originally appeared in *Mercy of Tides: Poems for a Beach House* (Salt Marsh Pottery Press)
"Casting Further Thoughts of Freedom into the Sea" originally appeared in *The Melic Review*
"Sighting" originally appeared in *Avocet*
"Letter from Charles Darwin to His Sister, Catherine" (Letter No. 1) originally appeared in *New Mexico Humanities Review*
"Letter from Charles Darwin to His Sister, Catherine" (Letter No. 2 and 3) originally appeared in *Writing the Future: Progress and Evolution* (The MIT Press)
"On the Orchard's Edge" originally appeared in *Avocet*
"Great White Heron" originally appeared in *The Trumpeter*
"The Bone" originally appeared in *Octavo*
"Indigo Bunting" originally appeared in *Southern Humanities Review*
"The Last Harvest" originally appeared in *Sou'wester*
"Coyote" originally appeared in *Utah Holiday Magazine* and then, revised, in *Sou'wester*
"Piñon Jays Drinking at Great Salt Lake" originally appeared in *Terrain.org: A Journal of the Built & Natural Environments*
"Lupus" originally appeared in *Canadian Bulletin of Medical History*
"Coming Into Premeditated Light" originally appeared in *Terrain.org: A Journal of the Built & Natural Environments*

Contents

A BODY OF WATER

A Body of Water	11
The Best Time for Reading Poetry	12
A Gathering	13
Casting Further Thoughts of Freedom into the Sea	14
Sighting	16
Groundwater	18
Gravity	19
Running the Rio Negro	20
Letter from Charles Darwin to	
His Sister, Catherine *Letter No. 1*	21
Letter from Charles Darwin to	
His Sister, Catherine *Letter No. 2*	24
Letter from Charles Darwin to	
His Sister, Catherine *Letter No. 3*	27

ON THE ORCHARD'S EDGE

On the Orchard's Edge	33
If a Spider Can	34
Great White Heron	35
The Bone	37
Ghost Stories in the Swamp	39
Stony Field	41
A Gap in the Mending Wall	42
The Cloud Drifters	43
Staff	44
Great American Chicken	46
The Egret, I Choose	47
Indigo Bunting	48

The Last Harvest

The Last Harvest	51
Coyote	52
Piñon Jays Drinking at Great Salt Lake	53
Who Prepares for the Raven?	54
Hiking the Summit	55
Lupus	56
Divorce	57
Thieving	59
Colorado	61
Coming Into Premeditated Light	62

A Body of Water

A Body of Water

Look, I said,
my mind is like a riverfall:
it crashes over boulders,
persuaded
by smoothing silt,
ecstatic in the swirling
rhythm of itself.

My soul is like a shallow sea:
silent above clear undertow,
sings fury
in the tempest's reign,
impassive in the shifting
current of the storm.

My breath is like a tidal pool:
it washes in from farther seas,
creates shoreline with
diurnal moon,
hypnotic in the respiring
motion of a wave.

Look, I said—
to the glorious waterfall,
cautionless to the reality
of gravity,

to the reflective island bay,
shelterless to the seasonal course
of nature's force,

to the random salt lagoon,
voiceless to the constant call
of lunar pull—

I apologize.

The Best Time for Reading Poetry

Is after the airline serves its plastic lunch,
after I've read the science column
in the *News*, or *Audubon's* essay—
where my mind is left meandering like a stream
in Hemingway's Michigan—and I forget
half of what I've read thinking
about how a cricket calls on chaos
to evade a diving bat, how a bat
sees in darkness by its own silent
scream, how one less cricket is
the darkness in the night. Then
when the Boeing engines level off, I slip
into the poems of Oliver, Galvin, and
Ammons: and I am flying low over broken
cattails, awakened by my reflection in a bayberry
pond, stretching these feathered robes
until I am sweeping the air from the face
of a dusky dune. And they are there,
watching over the frantic creation,
the sheets of paper left unfinished
in frustration, and the last scribbled word—
the finite ending. And I cannot
come back down, until the plane
touches solid ground.

A Gathering

Assateague's wind-littered beach
meets me, often, on violent mornings:
early spring, the limp crucifix

of tangled skate. Or the hard autumn
freeze on fallow fields. Today
I came across a hermit,

a combination of weathered shell
and invertebrate detail. Courting
the surf's edge, he contemplated

whelk, settled lightly
on battered carapace, and gorged.
As I approached the single

feast—intricate crab workings,
imprecise red claw and eyes—
he disappeared into undertow. As waves

like shipwrecks then crashed
in the crescendo of the scene,
minimal armies relished in their creel,

black-headed gulls were born
of drifting chicken bones, and I
turned toward my Olds
and felt the wind consume the sea.

Casting Further Thoughts of Freedom into the Sea

1.

Any idea of order
has passed
with the wildly colored parrots sailing
backwards over broken marsh.

Whirling wind reminds me that sound
travels faster underwater—
so I dive
the canal's depth,
into bluebrown darkness, through
the madness of tangled mangrove,

2.

but then he is gone.

As I rise
and drive myself sputtering
into the nautical light, water
covers everything:
car doors will not open,
pink fish swim
the new streams of our streets.

3.

Receding, I see now
the mudcats
burrowing into grey sludge,
the bromiliads drowning
in their original

delight, relentless fisherman casting
flies like diving swallows
along the far bank
of Kendall Drive.

We must work together, I heard,
as the silt
thickens, and aluminum johnboats shine
like silver-winged swans.

4.

We must work together
but somehow I cannot.

Silver marlin swim
to deeper oceans as schools
of amberjack lift the sandy floor.
Sworded barracudas wreak havoc
on an island
of soft-shelled crabs.
Mottled groupers scrape
caudal fins against whole cities
of barnacles. All the while

I am casting
further thoughts of freedom
into the sea.

Sighting

1.

I was at Big Sur, and
it was midday. The landscaped
groves of redwoods sloped

to cedar and shrubby cliff.
Botanists may condemn me,
but all plants looked alike—rosy

aloes, spiked quartzes, fleshy
greens and purples and reds
that bled into the sharp brown

rocks of ocean's edge.
But this is not about plants:
it's about that one sighting,

and racing painfully along
the broken ledge. It's about
a thousand miles of waves

and nothing, and then surfacing
as only a cetacean can: slow
and smooth and determined.

Cold and silent, she falls now
into nautical darkness, chasing squid
and mackerel, octopus and eel.

Cruising the heavy currents.
Sliding past the sandy cove and into
the dark night that is ocean.

2.

Did she call as I slipped,
knee-gnarled, into
the sea? Was it otters laughing

or gulls clashing or that sweet,
sweet harmony I heard in her voice?
Did she hear my cry

as undertow cast this silent
life into the organic bottom
of urchin and kelp?

3.

I pushed myself onto the line
dividing sea from land,
scraped the salty palms

of precipice, and tumbled into sleep.
Dreaming, she moved to me
in the wavering green light.

Waking, she moved from me
a lifetime caught dancing and singing
in the fertile waters of the Pacific.

Groundwater

Could be any river in a boy's
memory: the Mississippi ebbing

into brackish bayous,
or the Oklawaha's broken-backed

gators sliding ice-like
into the mud. Could be the Ohio

and every barge's passage,
or the Hayfork where none dare.

Or it could be the lack
of a river—the Salt and Tanque Verde.

The Cienega, Santa Rosa, Zuni.
And it could be washrock moving

nowhere in a hundred years—then
thirty miles in one ravaging

flood. It could be the coyote pelt
fenced along the wash's far side,

a pack devouring a hare, a prickly pear,
thornbush, black sage, creosote, desert

hail. Or it could simply be underground,
like veins within the thigh, where

all blood runs thick to the surface
carrying this scribbled note of poverty.

Gravity

This grasping for sunlight,
for water.

§

The aspen leaves collecting
like discarded coins
at the base of some ravine:
a river turning
over itself in a race
for the sea.

§

The sharp and heavy gathering
of boulders
forcing a new branch of Curecanti,
where brook trout slap
like butchers' hands
against the rocks.

§

The silted bay.

§

This uneven world, spinning
wildly through the starry brambles
of a universe expanding
and expanding.

Running the Rio Negro

Plying the dark waters, banded redfin
find only tangled rootstumps and displaced
detritus. Upriver, natives climb down
from treetops into labor: liquid bronze curves
in the shape of raw backs—eight or ten men
working at some crude machine. Severed layers
of timber are their handiwork, floating
like bloated bodies that bridge the banks.
In the hills behind them fruitstands burn
with the sweet smell of citrus, flushing scarlet
conures and black-tipped boars.
Where the smoke lifts, the river drags
until it reaches a curve, deadens, and suddenly
breaks, driving caiman below and kestrel above.
A single island disputes the flow—
crowned with plank walls where torches burn
oily as the guard's skin. When he climbs
to his post the whole forest is his view:
upriver and down, across canopy and blackened field
to a point where he stands, devoured.

Letter from Charles Darwin to His Sister, Catherine

Letter No. 1

21 January, 1832

My Dearest Catherine,

Passage to the Cape Verde Islands,
a minor stopover for the *Beagle*,
but a major one for myself.
Oh, if you could have seen my face—
the color of stitched linen at Downs
(where last I have seen either you or Susan).
How can I explain my misery at that time?
The tormenting waves, the incessant rocking,
always rising and collapsing
as my stomach did the same.
Fitzroy is a fine man,
as he would look in on me while
I lay idle at sick bay;
But Wickham, his first mate,
knew no friendship for me.
My quarters fare little better—
I share the poop cabin,
and have my drawers; the two others
(officers both) have lockers.

16 March, 1832

Finally it is Spring—
it seems as if even these vast seas
know the changes. They are richer,

though I knew well before we reached the mainland
we were there. A single leaf, a barkless twig,
a clod of saturated grass, still living—all signals.
No beauty exists in all the world
such as in these tropical lands.
In all my days of studying,
under Henslow or even Sir Adam Sedgwick,
I was never prepared for the absolute
numbers and grand diversity of life—
of species. I have been able to collect,
though I must have killed
hundreds of insects, small mammals, and birds.
(Do not worry, Catherine, I know how
you love life. These species are too numerous
for my sampling to harm.)

One butterfly must be named for you—
its wings are the majesty's blue blazoned
with scarlet, violet, and even silver.
How much it reminds me of your favorite brooch.
These lands have too many more to describe,
the brilliantly colored parrots, the gay
primates swinging on twisted branches...
Father must accuse me
of lizard-catching now, as well.

Yet in all of this beauty, one thing
remains disturbing. Here
on Bahia, on the Northeastern coast
of Brasil—chiseled into the delirious
greenness of rainforest—
man holds man captive.
Nothing plays enchanting in blood
mixing with sweat on the whip-cuts
of the negroes. Nothing enchanting
in the deep brown skin

chained with iron coils.
You must see the difference.
I collect a few specimens for knowledge,
for all—it is my passion, no man sees harm.
But these men, vulgar and cruel,
they act as if they transcend the Creator,
though He who created such solitudes
surely must not agree.

We depart for the South
in but a short while. I cannot say
I will be home soon—the Beagle
shelters my bed now, much as
the tropical canopy is secure in the mist.
You cannot know
unless you see these forests
and breathe this air...

With loving passage,
Charles

Letter from Charles Darwin to His Sister, Catherine

Letter No. 2

9 June, 1834

My Dearest Catherine,

Our course lays due south, a new passage
through the Straight
of Magellan, and I cannot fathom
what strange currents lurk
beneath the iron clouds. Once
I captured the alien
view of Southern glaciers:
inverted domes rimmed with purest
white (oh, how the stars must be jealous!);
but Catherine, it is their blue
which holds me.
Fitzroy remarked
these are the frozen flames of Vulcan,
though I questioned the atmosphere
and found other evidence: ice
crystals gathering and refracting
the light. A simple combination
of muted sky and sea.

Yet I fear this voyage
is leaving me too scientific—it is not
some chemical reaction or
ice cones permeated by tropospheric rays.
There is more; and
I can only say, when I see these glaciers,
I am reminded of mother's eyes.

Beneath heavy skies,
however, we are threatened
by harrowing winds and black
fingers of basalt.
These are unexplored waters,
so I am braced by the cartography, the geology—
yet I must fear
a wooden hull's limitations

28 July, 1834

Valparaiso!
We have anchored
(both our wind-tattered sails
and our restless feet) at the chief
seaport of Chile, the city
whose fragrances recall the intricate
tropical gardens of St. Cruz in Teneriffe.
And if the dense green
forests of Brasil cause your eyes
to ache, then Aconcaqua
and the long chain of Andes
will leave you blind!

I am reminded again
of the numerous species
which make up the grandeur of life:
I have seen, in the high
hills of Patagonia,
a bird larger in wingspan
than a British skiff's sails, and more
buoyant. I have seen on the uneven
playas of Tierra del Fuego a dumb and
flightless bird six hands higher than my brow.
And I have seen, weaving

the icy Antarctic waters, a slick
bird whose wings
are more efficient
than the finest pair of fins. And I have found
a striking likeness in their thin bones,
in dry feathers...
Every evening I ask the Creator,
How long are the days of the Genesis,
oh Lord? Yet I cannot discuss
such heresy with Fitzroy, who nearly abandons me
upon a lifeless rock in the Pacific;
but with you, I can leave
these questions, and more...

In loving passage,
Charles

Letter from Charles Darwin to His Sister, Catherine

Letter No. 3

9 October, 1835

My Dearest Catherine,

We have sailed from the anarchy
of Lima and Peru
for the drier anarchy of the Galapagos,
where volcanic craters burn
without lava—
their regular forms jutting
from the archipelago
like the great iron-foundries
at Staffordshire.
And though there are no plumes,
the slight vapour blends
with low sky so that once again
the world is gray.

It is gray in the mutinied captain's
skull found among salt-green
succulents, in the oppressive
heat of absent wind, and
in dusky hues of equatorial finches.
Perhaps it is my mood which is truly
gray, as Fitzroy turns
madder with the days
and crewmen yearn for British seas.

Yet we are here, among these
curious rocks, and surely there is hope
in their exploration.

25 October, 1835

What joy in the cloudless skies,
in these barren isles! Though I have found
few species, it is their rarity
which excites. On Albemarle,
the largest island, I have tossed
a remarkable lizard by tail into the sea.
And always he returns!
On Chatham Island
I have balanced unsteadily
upon the giant back of a tortoise grazing
the sweet red fruit of cactus!
And of thirteen species
of finch, where I was drowning
in the dullness of feather,
I now sail on the varied waves
of their beaks!
Come sail with me
Catherine—take the wind west
to these juvenile isles and dance
among the gray feathers
that make up the brilliance of life.
If I appear too drunk to write
with steady hand and level mind
it is because I am too
undernourished not to go on.
Though sailors laugh
as I sketch the remarkable shapes
flourished since just one finch
lit upon Indefatigable's jagged
beach, I am aware only of life's
ability to persevere,
and evolve.

But in man's own wilderness,
void of cottages and cobblestone
and into the saline deck
of navigator's ship, perseverance
usurps evolution, discarding it quite
entirely. No, you should not dance here.
Dare say that I should not, either—
but for these birds and vines
and islands. And the faint memory
of a distant home.

In loving passage,
Charles

On the Orchard's Edge

On the Orchard's Edge

I search for something, a glimpse
    like a tulip red will-o-wisp,
        that has just been found. On the dry

floor of apple leaves, his breast leaps out
    like a salmon climbing rapids, tiny feet
        clench an invisible branch, stained

glass eyes are now broken.
    As I bow, hands cupped, to lift
        the light body, dark snakes slide

through the grass, tasting the rosy scent
    of death, and glide toward the living bird
        that is my hand. I flutter

the broken wings of my fingers and watch,
    with chickadee and grackle alike,
        as my grosbeak enters the unhinged chapel

of snake's fragile jaw. I feel the terrible
    way in which the gray grass slowly
        unbends and the black ribbons twist

upon my hand, numb between the leaves.
    I feel the breached blood from my wrist
        drain into the bird and the muted

chorus of life in the thirsty air.
    And somewhere farther back, a low
        and empty song—the widowed mate,

my other desolate hand.

If a Spider Can

She spills her golden silk against the wind:
miles of drifting line

are free until, latching the broken reeds,
she is anchored. Perhaps the delicate

spider will catch a black fly, or a moth.
Perhaps midge or brown darner.

But in that chaotic beauty of web, the light
geometry of thread and wind,

there is more. She eyes the red-winged
blackbird. Her silver orbs focus on belted

kingfisher. She dances madly
on thoughts of gallinule.

Beyond the sawgrass a boy leans
against the wind as his kite climbs:

if the golden twine is long enough
perhaps he can tangle a gull.

Perhaps he'll snare the arcing jet.

Great White Heron

She is a ghost of her former bluegray
self, cautiously feeling
her way through mangrove
roots twisted upon themselves
like watersnakes held motionless in the wood.
I want to say she is a pale
Cleopatra, but then she calls—
scroawk scroawk—and one cry
reminds me she is queen only of marsh.

§

The cut of her eyes
is sharp as her tawny beak, quick
as the speared mullet she brings up
gasping through blood-red gills.
In one swift movement the fish
is flipped and swallowed headfirst—
to the surprise
of a thieving tropicbird
rising abruptly
before facing that spear.

§

When the heat of late summer stales,
she slips deeper into the shade
of a bald cypress stand and stares me
into submission.
And I step toward her,
lifting my reed-thin legs
through the braided roots.
Now I am spreading my dusty wings, coming

upon her as she raises that sharpened spear.
We twist our smooth necks
like branches beneath the waterline.
We move, eyes motionless
to the slow rhythm of rising waves.
And we dance, wings extended
to the reckless wind...

§

Waking, the great white heron
spreads her elegant wings
across the bay—
in the low cry that stills the air,
we vanish.

The Bone

Polished, the Neolithic prize
would gleam almost life-
like above the headboard.
Rough, it would rest silently
in the glass case of the middle hall.
This one is different: A long highway
of red channels up to the pinnacle,
to the femoral joint, like Old
Trochanter's Curve in one of those
sunsets so gruesome you
couldn't turn away until
the valley drank in the vermilion sun.
Under dimmest lantern, with wire
brush and quarter-inch chisel, I could
trace the trail, and wonder
what had traveled it, and when.
Now it rests against the articulated
smoothness of the dining table, across
a stretch of what appears to be ever-
black of ebony surface:
The joint at the upper end, a gloxinia
on the naked wood; the lower, smaller end
smooth as if no flesh ever
grew, no blood ever bled.
And the channel—groove up
like an I.V. straight through
my arm—searching parallel avenues
for my heart, and finding it
in slumber. Then draining the precious
red through a new detour,
now a part of me. A curse
has befallen me, and I will
be damned in some archaic

language if I destroy it, so
I hide it from my family—
deep within their nighttime world—
just down the hall. And in Unther
Hall at the Academy, colleagues dream
to touch my channel—divert it
from me, and drive straight off
Old Trochanter's Curve, flowering
down while my blood runs to the river.

Ghost Stories in the Swamp

There it is again—
black algae overripe,
or the oozing stench
of crappies cleaned
but never cooked.
It creeps steadily
out of Itchetucknee,
where the creek
loses itself among cypress
knees and cabbage palms.

We never saw it coming.

You've seen it,
etched against
your crimson shadow,
bleeding through planks
of juniper stripped
and left splintered
by a woodsman's polished axe—
your father's pride.

The backwaters never
promised a prize cut:
you couldn't even run
a mill saw past
Cripple Creek. But
you tried, and the papers
labeled you insane,
said your mind sank
with the graveled gears
and greaseless iron blades.

Yes, that stench is blacker
than the cottonmouth's
back, and now trails
are not traveled
since your frenzied night.

We never saw it coming.

You did—slow
as the bog petrifies,
fast as your
hatchet flash.

Stony Field

Whose fields are these I think I know…
How many times does that line go through my head as I walk this lowgrass place? How many times will I stop just short of that long stone snake, my father's wall? Why won't the poetry of Frost, or autumn's hard frost, release me from this curving hold?

Yet where else do smooth dark stones bud, like so many frozen potatoes, from the moist soil? I've wrestled three now from the ground, working my fingers around them, setting them delicately on the larger bulks of stone that intersect this field in perfect geometry. Almost.

The first one was the most difficult. Its egg-shaped top protruding from the wet grass, green as the evening sea, bluffed the size of my fist. Now its whole self, dimpled and patched with the dark and rich soil, proves triangular—big as late season pumpkin.

My second prize gave in easily, more like rootless stem than dense granite. Still, its oblong shape and perfect smoothness are admirable.

But it is the last stone that makes me kneel now to study its geologic past, its ecological present. Within it is a tight cavern, like a worm's staunch front door. Shall I pry? The fleshy worm of my finger may be too impersonal.

I lift the petrified load, turn the hole away, and shake. Unsteadily.

Two pebbles drop, and I lower their mother. The children, themselves smooth and gray, are twins. I roll them softly in my naked hand as a drop of rain marks my wrist. As I continue to examine the infants, the iron sky peels and cold water tumbles down. I look at the endless line of rocks—the wall—then back to my cupped hand. The pebbles are nearly floating.

Whose fields are these I think I know? The stones, it seems, have known all along. They hold fast.

A Gap in the Mending Wall

Something there is that doesn't love one
Who doesn't love a wall, that watches
From gaps between smooth-rolled stones,
And laughs when cold noses sniff, tickled by moss,
And bounce granite chunks with the wag of tail.
Mending-time brings out the devil in them,
And two neighbours as well. They gleam wistfully
At each other as the naked human hands practice
Ancient spellbinding—to teeter the "loaves"
That balance only under the presence of eyes.
There where the men, on either side, want the wall,
Regardless of need, they shall place it.
Something spies the common work, brings pain
To back, and twenty yards behind the men,
Calls wind to bring it down. One throws
Pine cones, the other rotten apples—
Until the back of head is knocked, and wrath
Replaces mischief; and the wall slumbers
Half built. "Gnomes," one man mocks
His target, and it is gnomes, exactly.
He can't say it for himself, he's swallowed
An apple core! And as the neighbour's stone
Savage crashes to the ground, he mumbles
Again and again, "Good fences make dead neighbours."

The Cloud Drifters

They are here, if anywhere,
settling like winter
over Snowbird Range

though the season is summer.
In morning, when western hills
are content to outgrow dawn's

shadows, their passage
is present. The spider knows,
nearly drowned in the design

of her web. The grass knows,
as the sun heats the drops
collected at split leaves.

Perhaps the hickory knows
best, submerged in its own
nautical light. Paths

etched along forest lines
call me into the hazy depth
that must be their home.

Yet when I push forward,
the sun quickens the air until
they are gone. So here

among pitched pine and
granite slides, hardwood shelter
and faltering fern, I will wait

in the blue shadow of the mountain:
the slow and smooth
coming of their infinite front.

Staff

Theirs is not a pillar
but some urban
structure twice the length
of my naked hand,
where viburnum leaves like great
gray sails drift upon a million
shining bodies,
a procession
of ants pushing forward.
The twisted stems,
the fractured latticework of vines—
these are their highways.

§

My brother was five
when he smothered their hidden
city: white arms and legs
appeared boneless
in three-alarm dance
as he shred his
clothes and sprinted
toward mother calling red-faced,
garden hose ready.
The insects' commonality,
my brother's body
of red hills and white
valleys, drew his true
hatred of ants,
and captured my horrible
fascination.

§

What leader says to his forces:
Bridge that chasm,
and the multitude of identity-
less bodies pulse forward
at the frayed end
of wood and swamp?
What chief asks of his tribe:
Make the other side,
form this living bridge
so that we may all cross?
And I say, make
the other side,
so that I might touch the splendid
silence of your march,
so I might lift you upon
this infinitely living staff.

Great American Chicken

I have seen more presentable birds—
the mallard with its teal-streaked
wing, or the indigo flash
of bunting. But this courting,
this long-grass dance with bellowed coo
and craning head and I think it was fire
on its chambered breast.
Who knows how long that passion
can light up the prairie sky?

The Egret, I Choose

Not because of his plumage, for the wood duck is no less
than a batik at the Indonesian hand of its creator;

not because of his flight, for the ruby-throated hummingbird
is simply more efficient;

and not because he wades water, for a company of plovers
presents a better show.

But because he stands still as the moon, and as white;
because the green-striped cichlids know certain fear

upon the rush of that golden spear;
because his darker cousin still waits patiently at the frayed

end of reedy pond;
and because he will sail the cracked back of crocodile;

and because there is no love lost in his piercing stare;
and because he is egret, remaining noble in the poorest of swamps;

and because she is egress, the exit he deserves.

Indigo Bunting

This is music, he said,
and his voice climbed
the thin ladder of air

like a cat chases moths,
tumbled like
the river desperate

in flood—his chest filling
with the thick
liquid of song. This

is music: not so much
the silver-chorded calls
or the silent intervals

of indigo flash
between yellowgreen limbs,
but the complete cessation:

the wind, the river, the earth's
core groaning
among its fiery teeth

to hear this simple song.

The Last Harvest

The Last Harvest

She was taught that river systems
tree branches & veins are all mathematically

equivalent That a skein of geese
is directed by the electromagnetic pull

of iron within the earth's core
That the brilliant wash of a sunset &

the enlargement of the harvest moon are due
simply to condensed particulates

in the atmosphere She was taught this
& believed it but wanted to learn further

why the geese shining in flight like a string
of pearls know the line of Old Hansen's

ranch the harvest moon lies swollen
against the starless sky & the dying

sun flares longest before the frozen night
Why the cottonwood's branches reach

highest above hidden stones
the Colorado's tributaries course dry

through her father's fields & the blue-red blood
in her mother's veins does not move at all

Coyote

I cannot follow the river of her myth.
Perhaps Papago, or Hopi.

In legend, she was born of the sharpest
cactus—the cholla—and spread her thin

roots into the desert soil.
She broke the underground river

and blossomed into life. As punishment,
the Great One gave her thickened fur,

and naked pups. Confined
to the desert,

she was weaker than the wolf,
could not hide like the fox,

took heavy heat from the white sun.
She ate the horned toad spitting blood

into her eyes, the gila monster leaking
venom through her veins, and the prickly pear shooting spears

through her tongue.
And she became strong.

I said, I cannot follow the river
of her myth; but I can

follow her sweet desert song
like a stream through the fiery hills.

Piñon Jays Drinking at Great Salt Lake

It was something in the heavy chatter:
how the gravelly calls

dropped, like the bluer than black
jays, to juniper. Something,

moreover, in the deliberate withdrawal of blood-
rich brine at the lake's white edge,

which recalls Cochiti.
In legend, when the feasting people

would not feed Old Salt
Woman, she gathered

the children beneath piñon
and changed them to jays.

At Santa Domingo
the pueblo people heard, and offering

to feed her, instead ate her flesh.
They called Rainmaker to wash

her away—him tumbling
like a riverfall—

and she became this great brackish lake.
Here now, the molting children

puncture her skin, drink
the salty blood and pray to drop dark

feathers, walking home like always
to begin the nightly feast.

Who Prepares for the Raven?

Job 38:41

Finding the wild-eyed dog
of my neighbor's yard,
the lion falls back
    into the dry wash—
    the barbed and broken scrub.

Finding the new light
of my lover's eyes,
our bodies curve back
    into the slough of the bed—
    the dark and driving surf.

By morning,
    we are nourished.

Hiking the Summit

Thirteen miles have passed beneath
these broken boots, though I
have been lost since the first step.
I cannot see snow-crowned
peaks or a canyon gone crazy
upon itself, but only my breath, thick
as frost on the evening ridge. As
the trail grows twisted, I lose level
ground and fall into a rushing spring,
the water drowning my call
with the taste of panic,
sweetness. I work the current
like a cutter through ice, reach
the bank to dream of sleep,
and fall upon the hardened earth.
As the moon slides across the frozen
sky, distant wolves hurl their calls
against my camp. Waking, I spur
simmering coals and return
the howls, watching as my fire
grows. When the flames
form a ladder, a straight line
of smoke opens the night.
I climb in, and the trail is gone.

Lupus

After the dry shell splits
and falls, my sister (the dark-
edged butterfly) rows her deep
blue wings of Japanese paper
into the thick liquid
of the dawn. Violet or perhaps
phlox—a flower familiar
as the bird-thin bones of her labored
hand—gives pause. She lands,
drinks from the pearl-fruited anther,
slips suddenly into the flat
palm of the wind. Mad
at herself for giving in,
she flutters wildly against
the branches hemming her like
a ribcage. Cracked and leaning,
the sternum splits and my sister
is speared. The disease finds
its way quickly through the light
cells of wings, body, spirit.
Rising, she crawls to the limb's
arthritic edge. Torn and dying,
she is the last brilliant leaf
on this failed and falling tree.

Divorce

I

When I became divorced
from my mother, the lawyers all
wore white—like the ceiling,

the walls. As they worked
out the details, pushing me
into a new life, I said

cut me so I will not dangle
like a curved leaf at the end
of a spider's thread.

And the curved blade,
the silver-quick hand
of the attorney, left me

to meet the father
I never knew I had, except
the murmur that was his voice.

II

When I became divorced
from my father, like a branch
stripped in a storm,

I lay there, still
alive, suddenly aware of the sharp grass
bearing my weight.

Nothing was said
through three odd marriages,
but I knew like continental

drift that a line formed
along our fault. We walked it,
hands tied by the ribbon

of alimony, until a woman
taught me to look straight
into the mirror, past my father's eyes.

III

When I became divorced
from myself, and stepped
onto the fragile tundra soil,

I began digging a grave
so the earth, piled,
would block the constant summer

light. The heavy sky,
under a bluff
of rain, was simply a veil

from within which my mother
and father could watch.
With the fault line stretched

like an umbilical cord still
uncut, and the shining silver
blade in my father's

hand, I too watched the earth
grow higher, then fell into
the heavy sleep of a newborn child.

Thieving

From the wire grass   resilience
From the white perch   balance
From the short-leaf pine   longevity
From the scrub oak   emigration
From the scrub jay   endeavor
From the ocelot   nurturing
From the deerfly   persistence
From the hyacinth   cleansing
From the dragonfly   agility
From the drosophila   translucence
From the black bear   strength
From the egret   nobility
From the aphid   appetite
From the striped bass   reflection
From the cowbird   cunning
From the gopher tortoise   domicile
From the vole   faith
From the mole   vigilance
From the mullet   voice
From the whip-o-will   song
From the mosquito   passion
From the deer   caution
From the tick   endurance
From the leopard frog   camouflage
From the pea   fertility
From the blackbird   shadow
From the osprey   vision
From the nine-lined skink   speed
From the crawfish   escape
From the owl   silence
From the glasswort   repetition
From the gar   boundary
From the fire ant   community

From the lichen   prosperity
From the limpet   inheritance
From the manatee   humor
From the bumblebee   humility
From the human   theft

Colorado

You cannot write the poem
of this place: rather

ask the mountain—
a deep shadow casting

trout that coil sine-
like beneath the ice.

Ask the wind—giving
snow squalls sudden life,

fallen elk slow death.
Ask the plateau—

its native dwellers dancing
the red fire into night,

a goshawk diving
through cry of cottontail,

columbines dropping cold
blue. Ask the bighorn

if you can find him,
the grizzly of San Juan,

the pale maned wolf
of Indian Peaks,

the mountain lion sprawled
above tender lamb.

Oh what is the geography
of this place that

we cannot define it?

Coming Into Premeditated Light

And up from Navajo myths, the sandstone
sliced a scar that is my back, then crumbled

into a geometry of broken pottery.
This could be a trail, but I've become confused

by the painted walls, the architecture of caves—
here a bighorn, there a rigid warrior.

Only the red paint of my blood has touched
these broken walls since the Indians sketched

their script. Now my brushwork has added
new verses—a riverfall cascading onto hunting

grounds, a large ram drowned by my fresh blanket.
Up there, Shiprock rises like a thousand broken spears,

but beneath the dust, their gods must have commanded
worship in the form of fire, canyon, sacrifice.

And now, tracing the faint steps of this
subterranean trail, I press myself

through the grimace of the cave's exit
and hear the grinding of black clay for the kiln,

the rhythm of the pre-hunt chant,
and the slow echo of stone chipping stone.

in memory of Ben Phillips